How To Create A Speech That Will Be Remembered

How to create a speech that will make your message be remembered forever!

"Practical, proven techniques that will help you to make your next speech a success"

Dr. Jim Anderson

Published by:
Blue Elephant Consulting
Tampa, Florida

Printed in the United States of America

Library of Congress Control Number: 2015918280

ISBN-13: 978-1519109262
ISBN-10: 1519109261

Warning – Disclaimer

The purpose of this book is to educate and entertain. This book does not promise or guarantee that anyone following the ideas, tips, suggestions, techniques or strategies will be hired. It is the discretion of employers if you will or will not be hired. The author, publisher and distributor(s) shall have neither liability nor responsibility to anyone with respect to any loss or damage caused, or alleged to be caused, directly or indirectly by the information contained in this book.

Other Books By
The Author

Product Management

- How Product Managers Can Learn To Understand Their Customers: Techniques For Product Managers To Better Understand What Their Customers Really Want

- How To Have A Successful Product Manager Career: The Things That You Need To Be Doing TODAY In Order To Have A Successful Product Manager Career

- Product Manager Product Success: How to keep your product on track and make it become a success

- Communication Skills For Product Managers: The Communication Skills That Product Managers Need To Know How To Use In Order To Have A Successful Product

Public Speaking

- Secrets To Planning The Perfect Speech

- Secrets To Organizing The Perfect Speech: How to organize the best speech of your life!

CIO Skills

- CIO Business Skills: How CIOs can work effectively with the rest of the company!

- Managing Your CIO Career: Steps That CIOs Have To Take In Order To Have A Long And Successful Career

- CIO Communication Skills Secrets: Tips And Techniques For CIOs To Use In Order To Become Better Communicators

IT Manager Skills

- IT Manager Budgeting Skills

- IT Manager Career Secrets: Tips And Techniques That IT Managers Can Use In Order To Have A Successful Career

Negotiating

- Preparing For Your Next Negotiation: What You Need To Do BEFORE A Negotiation Starts In Order To Get The Best Possible Deal

- How To Open Your Next Negotiation: How To Start A Negotiation In Order To Get The Best Possible Outcome

Miscellaneous

- Power Distribution Unit (PDU) Secrets: What Everyone Who Works In A Data Center Needs To Know!

- Making The Jump: How To Land Your Dream Job When You Get Out Of College!

Acknowledgements

Any book like this one is the result of years of real-world work experience. In my over 25 years of working for 7 different firms, I have met countless fantastic people and I've been mentored by some truly exceptional ones. Although I've probably forgotten some of the people who made me the person that I am today, here is my attempt to finally give them the recognition that they so truly deserve:

- Thomas P. Anderson
- Art Puett
- Bobbi Marshall
- Bob Boggs

Dr. Jim Anderson

This book is dedicated to my wife Lori. None of this would have been possible without her love and support.

Thanks for the best 21 years of my life (so far)...!

Speaking.   Negotiating.   Managing.   Marketing.

Table Of Contents

What's The Best Way Give A Great Speech?

I'm pretty sure that we can all agree on one thing: we'd like the next speech that we give to be a great speech. Now the big question that we are all faced with is just exactly how to go about making this happen?

The one thing that will make any speech appeal to an audience is if we include a great story in it. However, we've got to have a way to figure out what the best story that we can include would be. Every speech that we are asked to give is different, but keynote speeches are the most visible. The good news is that there is a very specific way to go about making this type of speech.

An audience want's to know more about the person who is addressing them. Specifically, they often want to know about the bad things that have happened to you and how you have dealt with them. We get some help in figuring out how to communicate things like this if we go to the pros for help. Jack Welch's speech writer is one person who can lend us a hand.

When we want to write the perfect speech, we need to have the creative ideas that will make it a great speech. Sometimes no matter how hard we try, we just run out of ideas. This is when it becomes time to go read a book. If you are given a short amount of time in which to deliver your speech, you need to very carefully plan out what you'll say. The one thing that you don't want to do in any speech of any length is to use naughty words.

Stories are so powerful that we really should always be looking to include them in any speech that we give. This includes business presentations. However, we need to be careful about how much personal information we include in our stories because it is possible to include too much.

For more information on what it takes to be a great public speaker, check out my blog, The Accidental Communicator, at:

www.TheAccidentalCommunicator.com

Good luck!

- Dr. Jim Anderson

About The Author

I must confess that I never set out to be a public speaker. When I went to school, I studied Computer Science and thought that I'd get a nice job programming and that would be that. Well, at least part of that plan worked out!

My first job was working for Boeing on their F/A-18 fighter jet program. I spent my days programming fighter jet software in assembly language and I loved it. The U.S. government decided to save some money and went looking for other countries to sell this plane to. This put me into an unfamiliar role: I started to meet with foreign military officials and I ended up having to give speeches in order to explain what my product did.

Time moved on and so did I. I found myself working for Siemens, the big German telecommunications company. They were making phone switches and selling them to the seven U.S. phone companies. The problem was that the switches were too complicated. Customers couldn't tell the difference between one complicated phone switch from another complicated phone switch. Once again I found myself standing in front of the room giving speeches in order to explain what these complicated machines did and why ours were better than anyone else's.

I've spent over 25 years working as a product manager for both big companies and startups. This has given me an opportunity to do many, many presentations for customers, at conferences, and everywhere in-between.

I now live in Tampa Florida where I spend my time managing my consulting business, Blue Elephant Consulting, teaching college courses at the University of South Florida, and traveling to work with companies like yours to share the knowledge that I have about how to create and deliver powerful and effective speeches.

I'm always available to answer questions and I can be reached at:

Dr. Jim Anderson
Blue Elephant Consulting
Email: jim@BlueElephantConsulting.com
Facebook: http://goo.gl/1TVoK
Web: **www.BlueElephantConsulting.com**

"Unforgettable communication skills that will set your ideas free..."

Create Speeches That Motivate Your Audiences And Get Your Message Heard!

Dr. Jim Anderson is available to provide training and coaching on the topics that are the most important to people who have to speak in public: how can I create a speech that people want to hear and how can I deliver in a way that will allow me to connect with my audience and get my point across to them?

Dr. Anderson believes that in order to both learn and remember what he says, speakers need to laugh. Each one of his speeches is full of fun and humor so that what he says "sticks" with everyone.

Dr. Anderson's Public Speaking Training Includes:

1. How to plan your next speech: pick your purpose and understand your audience.
2. What's the best way to get PowerPoint and Keynote to work with you, not against you?
3. What do you need to do when you are presenting in order to truly connect with your audience?

Dr. Jim Anderson presents over 100 speeches per year. To invite Dr. Anderson to speak at your event, contact him at:

Phone: 813-418-6970 or
Email: jim@BlueElephantConsulting.com

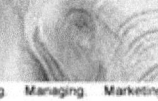

Blue
Elephant
Consulting
Speaking   Negotiating   Managing   Marketing

12

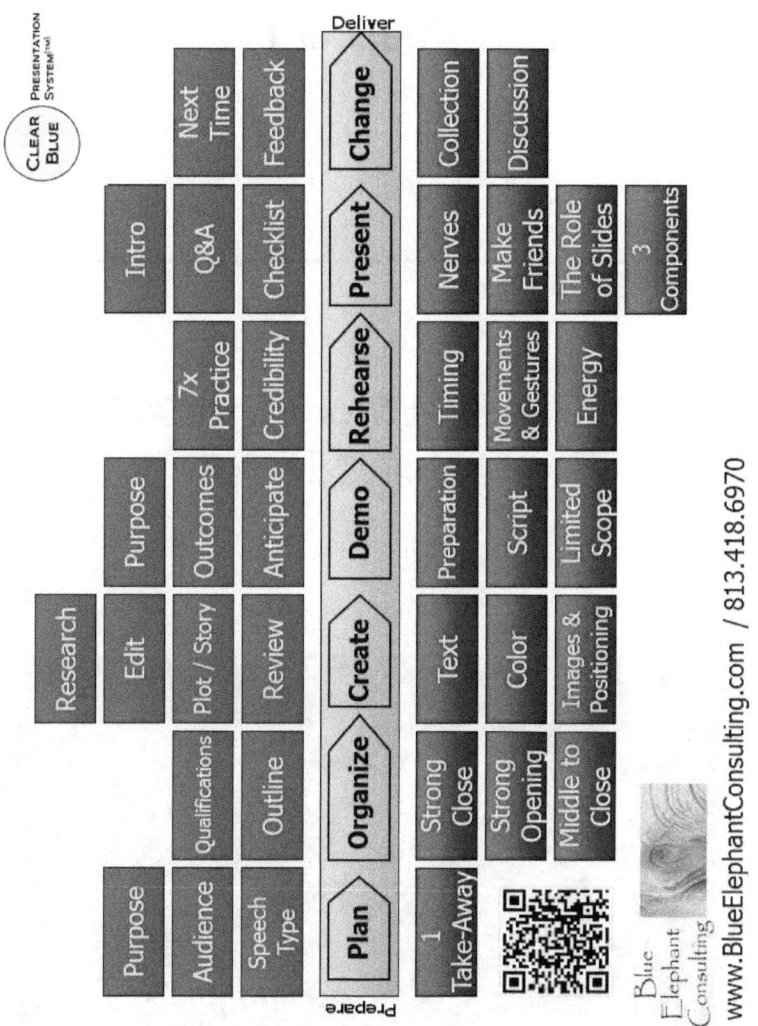

Blue Elephant Consulting has created the **Clear Blue™** presentation system for creating and delivering powerful and memorable presentations. The contents of this book are based on lessons learned during the development of the Clear Blue system. Contact Blue Elephant Consulting to learn more about the Clear Blue presentation system.

Chapter 1

What's The Best Story That A Public Speaker Can Tell?

Chapter 1: What's The Best Story That A Public Speaker Can Tell?

Oh, this one's an easy question to answer: your story. I don't care if you are giving a speech about the company's 3rd Quarter profits, or telling an audience about the best way to water-proof a roof, if you work a personal story into your speech it will instantly become a memorable speech. Now with that being said, if you do a bad job of working your personal story into your speech you will probably bore your audience to death. Hmmm, I wonder what the secret to doing this correctly is...

The first thing that you need to realize is that if you just up and tell a personal story, the odds are that it'll fall flat. Although we might think that every story we have to tell is a great tale, this simply is not the case. Instead, your story needs to be taken out, sharpened, and perhaps even polished just a bit before you tell it to an audience. One way to get things started is to sit down and just write / type it all out. Don't hold back here, just make it as long as it wants to be. Capture your story of overcoming a challenge, fighting a setback, dealing with a health issue, bad relationship, or financial disaster in all of its glory. Remember, your audience was not there so you need to remember what it felt like and communicate what all of your five senses were feeling.

Once you have it all written down, now is the time to start to shape it. Your story needs a good clear opening. Let your audience know why this is important. You also need to be aware of just how much time you have for your speech and your story within your speech. You'll need to trim it down to fit the time available.

Once you've got your personal story sorta looking like it's ready for prime time, now is the time to do some extra checking in order to make sure that it really is a good story to tell. The first thing that you can do is to be very clear about where and when your story took place. Instead of saying "back when I was in college" instead you need to say "12 years ago..." This will allow your audience to better identify with your story.

We all love movies and we're use to watching them. Just like a movie, your personal story will "play" better if you are able to tell it as a series of connected scenes. Your words will paint scenes in your audience's minds and these images will then blend together to create a complete movie of your story for them.

Create some drama by telling your story just like you felt it. If you hold back on some information and allow the audience to discover it just as you did, the tension in the room will quickly start to rise. The good thing about creative tension is that it means that your audience will be hanging on your every word.

Finally, you need a great conclusion that brings your audience back into the here and now. One way to do this to take just a moment and explain why the story that you told was so important to you. What did it all mean to you? Your personal story is yours and yours alone. You never have to worry about someone else telling it because it's all about you. Good luck in adding a personal story to your next public speaking opportunity and making it unforgettable!

Chapter 2

Just How Does One Create A Keynote Presentation?

Chapter 2: Just How Does One Create A Keynote Presentation?

Tis the season for college graduations and I was recently asked to deliver a keynote speech as part of an engineering graduation ceremony. The interesting thing about this speaking opportunity was that I was basically starting from ground zero – I didn't have an engineering keynote speech in my bag of tricks. This meant that I needed to build one from the floor up quickly – they asked me just a week before the big day.

As I was pulling together my keynote, it dawned on me that lots of presenters often find themselves in a similar situation and may not know how to go about creating a keynote speech that will fit the occasion. In an effort to fill this knowledge gap, I'm going to share with you the steps that I went through to build my keynote speech and, because I delivered it last night, I can also give you some feedback on what worked and what didn't.

1. **Always Start With Your Audience:** I followed this rule! I realized that I was going to be talking to a group of graduating engineering students, some of their parents, their professors, and various other people (dates, administrators, etc.). This gave me a fairly homogeneous group and that meant that I needed to work "engineering" content into my speech so that they would feel as though I was talking directly to them.

2. **Start At The End:** What's the purpose of a keynote? You probably aren't going to change any lives so you had better make sure that you don't try to. In my case, I decided that I had two goals: to entertain and to provide motivation for the graduates to succeed as they moved forward ("We know that you can do it").

3. **Content Is King:** So what to say? Since I knew that I was not going to be changing any lives with my speech, I decided to focus on two things: funny stories that have happened to me during my career and a discussion about what things the graduates needed to be aware of in order to have a great career. I mixed in several references to paying off student loans (everyone has those), homework (all engineers have too much of that), and dealing with professors. These were common elements that everyone could relate to.

4. **Watch The Clock!:** Early on I asked how much time I had for my keynote. I was told that 20 minutes would be perfect. It turned out that this was very important – I shaped my entire speech to fit in this time. It is instant death to the speaker who goes on too long especially in an after-dinner speaking situation like this was. People speak at about 150 words/minute and since I was going to be speaking for 20 minutes I knew that I had to limit myself to about 3,000 words which meant that I needed to…

5. **Write It Out!:** There is some controversy to this point, but here goes it anyway: I wrote my speech out from start to finish. There were two reasons that I did this. The first was to make sure that I could fit my speech into the 20 minute window – my written speech needed to be no more than 3,000 words long. The next was because I could remember reading somewhere that if you want to deliver a memorable speech, then you need to get your wording just perfect ("I have a nice thought" vs. "I have a dream"). In order to do this you need to write the speech out word for word. So I did it. Then I proceeded to revise it 1,000,000 times.

6. **Memorize It!:** So if you are never supposed to write out your speech, then of course you should never memorize

it! However, that is basically exactly what I ended up doing. I practiced my speech over and over reading it as it was written. After about 5 times of doing this, I was able to spend more time looking at my (pretend) audience than looking at my written speech. Did I ever completely memorize my speech, no. I did get it stuck in my brain well enough so that I really only used my written out speech as an occasional reminder. This mean that I spent most of the speech making eye contact with my audience.

7. **Use BIG Print**: For the version of my written out speech that I had before me when I was delivering the speech, I made some changes to the written out speech. I increased the font size to a nice, easy to read 16 point Arial. I then turned every sentence into its own bullet point. Needless to say this resulted in a longer printed speech – it was 13 pages long in its final form! Oh, make sure that you put PAGE NUMBERS on each page of your printed speech – you just know that you'll drop the whole thing as you walk to the podium!

8. **A Highlighter Is Your Friend**: As I read over my 13 pages of bulleted sentences, I found it difficult to keep my place. I ended up using a highlighter to highlight the one or two words in each sentence that were the key idea. This allowed my eyes to dance from highlighted word to highlighted word and that helped me to keep my place better.

9. **PowerPoint Can Be Your Friend**: I'm really good looking, but 20 minutes is a long time for an audience to spend staring at me. Since PowerPoint slides were already being used as a part of the graduation dinner, I decided to create some to use as part of my keynote. I ended up creating just 10 slides and none of them contained any words – each just contained a single

photo. As I delivered my speech, I had written out **[man with truck slide]** and so I knew when to move to the next slide. Each slide reflected what I was talking about at the time in my speech so the two media, spoken word and displayed image, helped each other. Oh, and I have a Kensington wireless remote control device that I used to automatically advance to the next slide – much smoother than having to run over and hit the space bar (or say "next!")

10. **Have A Good Ending:** Ultimately, this is what will stick in everyone's memory. I took some extra time and carefully worded my last few sentences so that everyone would feel a warm glow of congratulations for the graduates and they would feel as though they had been recognized for their achievements.

So how did it all turn out? I'd give myself a score of 90/100. The PowerPoint pictures that I used were very well received (here is one with a guy and a truck so you can see what they were laughing at) and so I probably should have used more of them. I explained how Milton Bradley's "The Game of Life" had good lessons for all of us and that went over fairly flat (not enough laughs). I would make changes if I ever gave this speech again, but I received lots of compliments. Making a speech to engineers interesting AND funny is no simple task!

Chapter 3

Why Your Audience Wants Bad Things To Have Happened To Their Presenter

Chapter 3: Why Your Audience Wants Bad Things To Have Happened To Their Presenter

Today's audiences are a jaded bunch. In fact, a Gallup Poll shows that just 16% of us have a favorable opinion of business executives. With all of the Wall Street failures and auto maker bailouts that are currently going on, this number will probably keep going down. What's a presenter to do in order to cut through the fog of cynicism that we are all existing in?

One way that presenters are doing this is by sharing their own stories of adversity. These stories seem to be able to reach out to audiences and somehow make the presenter much more "real" than just another glib business success story.

If this is what your audience wants, what can you do to meet their needs? We all may not have survived a wild bear attack, but we may be able to find other types of material in our lives that will allow us to connect with our audiences:

- **Audiences Love Adversity:** The bigger the challenge that you faced, the more they love it. Erik Weihenmayer is a mountain climber who is blind. He overcame lots of adversity and ended up climbing Mt. Everest. His story shows his audience how to overcome adversity in their lives.

- **Tales Of Survival Match Today's Business Environment**: Today's business environment is harsh and unforgiving and surviving is what most of your audience is trying do every day. Trisha Meili was assaulted and left for dead in New York's Central Park. She now speaks to audiences about what she had to go through in order to recover.

- **Find The Metaphor:** What your audience is really looking for is hope. They will be interested in your story no matter what you tell them, but it will have a real impact if they can understand that what you went through is similar to what they are currently going through. The fact that you survived (and hopefully thrived) is what is going to give them the courage to keep on trying.

- **Tie Your Story Into Business:** A great story will keep your audience on the edge of their seats – but what happens when you stop talking? John Amatt survived a mountain climb 20 years ago that killed three of his climbing teammates. The only way that he survived that disaster and made it to the top of the mountain was to make radical changes to his climbing route and tactics. This story is very well received by business people who are facing major changes in their business environments.

- **Use Humor Where Appropriate**: These topics can be pretty heavy – life and death struggles are rarely something that anyone wants to joke about. That being said, if your entire presentation is dark and scary, then your audience will just be happy when it's all over. Instead, use humor at the start and at the end in order to start and end on a lighter note. You audience will appreciate it and this will allow your message to sink in further.

We have not all faced life threatening situations. However, what your audience is really looking for is a good story that they can relate to. If you look back over your life, I'm sure that you can find points in which you were faced with a challenging situation that looked impossible at the time. Then all you have to do is weave a story that will grab your audience's attention...

Chapter 4

What Jack Welch's Speech Writer Can Teach Us

Chapter 4: What Jack Welch's Speech Writer Can Teach Us

So just about everyone out there knows who Jack Welch is – he was the CEO and Chairman of GE who lead them from a market valuation of $14B when he took over to a valuation of over $410B when he stepped aside. What many people may not know is that Jack is a great communicator.

Bill Lane who was Jack Welch's speech writer for over 20 years while he was at GE has written a book called Jacked Up: The Inside Story of How Jack Welch Talked GE into Becoming the World's Greatest Company. In it, Lane spills the beans on just how Welch got to be so good at getting his message across.

Probably the most important lesson that Jack Welch taught his speech writer was that self-confidence was the #1 attribute of a leader. With self-confidence you could go out and do nearly anything that you put your mind to. Now this was truly impressive when you realize that Welch had started out as a guy who both stuttered and was very shy. Needless to say, in the beginning Welch HATED to speak in public.

The speeches that were being given at GE when Welch took over were the standard types of speeches that you hear at any company gathering: boring reports on the success of such and such a team / department / division. One day while coming up with the list of speakers for an internal event, Welch called a stop to everything. He spent a few moments thinking to himself, and then he announced that going forward all speeches would be ones that told people what they ought to be doing.

From that point on in GE, everything was changed. All speeches needed to contain a learning point, a warning to others, some sort of insight, or something useful like a new technique or the speech didn't get made.

There was an amazing side benefit to this new speech policy. Almost across the board the presenters at these internal events became much better speakers. Why? Probably because they knew that they had something interesting to say. When they knew that the audience was going to be interested in what they had to say, they were filled with self-confidence and this just naturally made them better speakers.

So what does all of this mean to us accidental communicators? Simple, we need to stop giving boring speeches that are simply reports on what we've been doing. Instead, we need to look inside ourselves and discover what our audiences really want to hear about.

Keep in mind, what people want to hear most are your stories. The stories that tell them what you know, what you have done, what you have seen, and what they might find useful in some way. Not only are your stories interesting to them, but hearing a story also helps people to remember and retain what you have told them. Instead of having your message go in one ear and out the next, now it will actually stick!

Lane makes one final point in his book: Jack Welch always insisted that speakers give their audience the very best of their thinking. If you can do this, then your audience will respond by taking your message to heart.

Chapter 5

Hey Officer, Book That Presenter...

Chapter 5: Hey Officer, Book That Presenter...

We spend a lot of time talking about how to deliver your message verbally to your audience. However, there's a lot more to communications than just the spoken word. For your typical do-it-once-and-it's-over internal business presentation, the actual delivery is enough – do it well and then move on. But what about those presentations that you REALLY care about – the ones in which you'd like to change the world...?

There's a lot of different ways to make your presentations have a life after you've gotten done giving them. Podcasts, videos, etc. are cheap and easy to do these days. However, I think that if you are really trying to get your message across, then the written word is your most powerful tool. That my friend means that you just might have to write a book...

Write a book you say? Not me! I'm no J.K. Rowling or Steven King. Hey, you don't have to be – you just have to have something interesting to tell your audience and the words will flow out of you.

Neil Chethik is a published author who also works with others to help them get their books published. If you really care about the message that you are trying to communicate, then perhaps we need to spend just a few moments listening to what Neil has to tell us about getting a book published.

If you care enough about your message, then Neil says that there are three things that you need to think about when you are writing things down:

1. What is going to make your book unique (there are a lot of other books out there!)

2. What makes you so special that you are the best person to write this book (you are the best person, now figure out why...)

3. What are you going to do to make this book appear to have value for the audience of readers that you want to buy or obtain this book?

If you can make sure that your writing answers all three of these questions, then you are getting close having a published book. Once you have poured your heart out onto the (electronic) pages before you, the next step is to get yourself published.

Thankfully, Neil is once again here to help us out. He points out that here in the 21st Century there are a number of ways to get your message/book published. It's actually pretty easy to publish a book yourself. Somewhat tellingly this is called "vanity publishing". However, let's spend some time talking about the more difficult road to traditional publishing.

Neil tells us that here's what you are going to have to do in order to get the attention of a traditional publisher:

1. **Do Some Research:** off you go to your local Borders store. Find out where your book, once published, would be displayed. See what's already there. How would your book be different? Make sure that it would be different!

2. **Propose!**: Create a 10-25 page (double spaced) business proposal that tells a prospective publisher why they should publish your book. It's good to get help on this and the book How to Write a Book Proposal is a good place to start.

3. **Do You Need An Agent?**: This one is pretty simple – if you want one of the 25 biggest publishing companies to publish your book, then you need an agent. If you can

live with being published by a smaller shop or a university press, then you can just send your book proposal to them directly.

4. **Pick An Agent**: book agents get about 15% of anything that you make. Just like when finding a real estate agent, pick carefully.

5. **Personalize It**: After you've picked the agent that you want, create a personalized letter to include with the manuscript that you are sending to them. It has to make them want to read your manuscript – make it interesting and watch your spelling!

6. **Get A Lawyer!**: Because I know that you are going to be successful, please get a lawyer BEFORE you sign any agreement with an agent. You don't want to get taken to the cleaners here!

Chapter 6

When Presenters Run Out Of Ideas, It's Time To Read A Book

Chapter 6: When Presenters Run Out Of Ideas, It's Time To Read A Book

Sometimes when we are called on to give a presentation, we sit down to create the presentation only to find that our creative juices have somehow run dry. Oh, oh – this can be a big challenge. What always just seemed to "be there" can go missing just when we really need to draw upon it. What's a presenter to do?

Despair not fellow presenters! This situation has happened to me and other presenters and we have a fairly simple solution that will get you out of this pickle: read a book.

Katherine Meeks is a New York City based speech consultant and language coach. She's spent a lot of time with speechwriters and has made a not-so-amazing discovery: those of us who read a lot seem to have the best thoughts, the best style, and the most precise ways of using our vocabulary to make our presentations memorable.

I can hear you now: "Hey, I have a subscription to People magazine – I'm well read!" Umm, nope that's just not going to cut it.

How often do you work on expanding your vocabulary? Probably not all that often. It turns out that once we are out of school, the size of our vocabulary stops growing as fast as it once did. Reading turns out to be one of the most effective ways that as adults we can continue to grow our vocabulary. Once again, a word-of-the-day desk calendar is not going to get you to where you want to be.

If you want to become a great presenter, then you have to become a great reader. In order for this to happen, you need to discover interesting books. The best way to do this is to simply ask other people that you know what they are reading. The key here is to find a way to filter the unending stream of books that are produced every year into a manageable trickle that you can have a chance of reading.

Other good ways to fete possible books for you to read include seeing movies and then reading the book. I was touched by the movie "Pursuit of Happyness" and just had to follow this up by getting and reading Chris Gardner's book that the movie was based on. Wow – the book was much different from the movie, I was very glad that I read it. Another way to pick out the books that you might want to read is to spend some time with the book review section of your local newspaper – this can be a great way to spot stinkers.

Once you've created a list of books / authors that you'd like to read in order to have your presentations become inspired, the next thing that you need to do is to get your hands on some books. This is actually quite easy to do, but you've got to remember that you've got a lot of choices. Remember when you used to go to the library as a kid? Well guess what – the library is still there. When was the last time that you went?

Other sources for books include your local used book store (why pay full price?), the local Borders / Barnes & Nobel, and your on-line friend – Amazon. It really doesn't matter where you get your books from, just make sure that you get them and that you read them! Your audiences will thank you...

Chapter 7

How To Write The Perfect Speech

Chapter 7: How To Write The Perfect Speech

Last week I had the opportunity to give the perfect speech. Now, you might be offended by this statement and are probably wondering just how I could become so full of myself, so perhaps I should explain myself. I had spoken in this venue four times before, I had been invited to speak again because they liked what I had had to say before, and I knew that I was going to be speaking about a month before I actually got up on stage. These are all the elements of a perfect speech.

Since I already basically knew what I wanted to tell this audience, this time around I really worked on HOW I said it – I wanted to make an impact in their lives. A while ago I had read an article in which Patricia Fripp boiled down what makes a really memorable speech: tell a story, make your point, tell a story, make your point, etc.

So I did. I ended up working six stories into my speech and then following them up with the point that I wanted to make. In order to make sure that I would fit into the 30 minutes that I had been given, I did some quick math: 30 minutes x 150 words/minute = 4,500 words in speech. I then did something that I've almost never done before.

I wrote out my speech word for word. I did this because I had read somewhere else that in order for you to "tune" a speech, you need to know exactly what you are going to say. This came out to be about five single spaced pages of text.

Chapter 8

How To Make Your Two Minutes Count

Chapter 8: How To Make Your Two Minutes Count

When you speak to an audience, how long do you talk for: 60 minutes, 30 minutes, 10 minutes? Any of these are normal answers. What would you do if you only had two minutes to get your point across?

In my neck of the woods, a developer wants to build a gas station at the entrance to my neighborhood. There are good sides and bad sides to such development, but the neighborhood has decided that this is not something that they want to happen.

The way that you stop things like this from occurring is that you go down to city hall and attend a zoning hearing. At this hearing both sides get to present their sides and a hearing master will end up making a decision. The trick is that both sides were limited to 15 minutes of talking. Lots of people wanted to voice their objections so I was looking at having only 2 of those 15 minutes in which to speak. What could I say in order to have an impact?

When I sat down to get ready to figure out what I would say, I realized that I was dealing with no more than about 300 words (150 words /min x 2 min = 300 words). I knew that I needed to throw in some facts and stats for the zoning hearing master, but then I also needed to come up with some sound bites that any reporters who were attending could use as quotes.

So what did I come up with? You be the judge if any of these would stick in your mind if you hear them:

- If this gas station is permitted to be built, the zoning laws will have to be changed in order to account for the mountain of roadside memorials that will appear due to drunk drivers.

- The County might be tempted to change zoning rules in order to generate more revenue ; however, just like a teenager who gets a tattoo this would be a bad idea that the County would end up having to live with forever.

- A gas station that is open 24-hours a day and which is located close to a major highway will act like a bug light for all manner of criminals who are seeking an easy score.

The next day one of my "image statements" was quoted in the local paper. Not too shabby for a two minute speech!

Chapter 9

Presenters Who Use Naughty Words –
Good Or Bad?

Chapter 9: Presenters Who Use Naughty Words – Good Or Bad?

If you are under 18 (or if you were at one time), please cover your ears as you read these words.

Let's talk about **naughty words**. What words do I mean you say? I'm talking about all of the common ones like $^!, *&@^, &%$#, and of course &#&@. Just for good measure we should also throw in some of the up-and-coming modern phrases like $&^%$#@!%&.

If you watch TV, go to the movies, listen to top 40 music, or even read books that are on the top seller lists then you are being exposed to what we can call "offensive language" all the time. The big question is if there is so much of this in our daily lives, **can we now start to work it into our presentations**?

I say that the answer is "**no**". I believe that there are several reasons why.

Gene Perret was Bob Hope's head writer for 12 years and he's spent a lot of time thinking about the use of street language in comedy and presentations. I agree with a lot of what he has to say.

The #1 reason why presenters should not use offensive language in our presentations is because it is the equivalent of **taking the easy way out**. Offensive words shock our audience when they hear them. It's the same as if you zapped them with an electrical charge. However, it's momentary and then it's gone. It's much harder (and more fulfilling) to use non-offensive words to capture and hold their attention.

Here's an example: once upon a time Winston Churchhill was at a party when a woman who didn't like him came up to him and said "Winston, if I were your wife, I would poison your tea." Churchill responded by saying "Well, you can just go $%#@ yourself". Oh, wait. No he didn't. Instead, what he said was **"Madam, if I were your husband, I would drink it."** If he had responded the first way, this incident would have been quickly forgotten. However, because of the words that he did use, it has been remembered to this day.

So the next time you are crafting a speech and you're tempted to throw in some street language just to show how hip and cool you are, don't. Instead spend the time and find a way to instead show your audience **how memorable you can be**.

Chapter 10

Business Stories:
Out Of Place Or On Target?

Chapter 10: Business Stories: Out Of Place Or On Target?

One question that I keep getting asked over and over by speakers that I am working with is if storytelling is such a powerful communication tool, then **why isn't it used more in business settings**? It's a good question, but the answer is a little bit complicated.

Where Did All The Stories Go?

I can't tell you how many business presentations I've sat though that at the end I couldn't have told you what was talked about if my life depended on it. It's not that the speaker was necessarily bad, it's just that nothing that they said caught my imagination and so **nothing stuck**.

This is where stories come in – people remember stories long after you get done talking. We remember them because it's a **fundamental way** that humans have exchanged information for as long as we've been around.

For some reason, people have decided that stories don't have a place in the environment of business – perhaps they don't think that they are "**grown up**" enough and that facts and figures should only be used. This is completely wrong.

What Is The Value Of A Business Story?

Dr. Caren Neile has been looking into the use of stories in the workplace and she reports that Makingstories.net president Terrence Gargiulo has identified **9 key values** to using a story in a business presentation:

1. They empower the speaker.

2. They can be used to create a particular environment.
3. They can be used to bond individuals together.
4. They can help your audience to engage in active listening.
5. They can be used to resolve differences between both individuals and groups.
6. They can encode information.
7. They can act as tools to help with brainstorming.
8. They can be used as weapons.
9. They can be used to start or enhance a healing process.

The professional storytellers define the act of storytelling as being "... *a face-to-face oral narrative that employs non-verbal communication and imagination*". One side effect of this definition is that when stories are told in a live business setting, they are **much more powerful** than when they are just written down.

What Kind Of Stories Work In Business Presentations?

Dr. Neile reports that Annette Simmons, who is the president of the company Group Process Consulting, believes that there are **six types** of stories that can be used in a business environment:

1. **Who I Am**: this type of story is used to gain an audience's trust by having the speaker explain where they are coming from.

2. **Why I Am Here**: this story type is a way to communicate your agenda to your audience.

3. **The Vision**: this story paints a vision of the future that the audience can see and can then decide that they want to be a part of it.

4. **Values-In-Action**: this story shares the good things that can happen when the audience has shared values and the bad things that can happen when those values are violated.

5. **I Know What You Are Thinking**: this story shows how connected the speaker is to the audience and that he/she has their best interests in mind.

How Can We Use Stories During Business Presentations?

Stories that your audience **can relate to** are the best kind of stories to use. This means that you need to spend the time to uncover the true stories that already exist within the organization: the successes, the failures, and people behaving both badly and wonderfully.

The power of business stories is that they provide one of the most effective ways to achieve agreement about how to resolve issues and meet goals. It's no longer a question of **IF** they should be used, but rather a question of **HOW MUCH** they should be used.

Chapter 11

Personal Information: How Much Should A Presenter Reveal?

Chapter 11: Personal Information: How Much Should A Presenter Reveal?

Have you ever sat through a dry and boring speech? Of course you have, we all have. Did you spend any time trying to figure out why the speech was so dry? I'm going to bet that at least one of the reasons is that the speaker didn't connect with the audience was because the speech content itself was impersonal. Did you know that it's possible for a speaker to go too far in the other direction also?

A Speech That Nobody Wants To Hear

Once upon a time I had the misfortune to attend a speech that was being given by a presenter who had been married four times. Now the fact that he had been married so many times was no big deal, but the speech was on how to choose the correct investment plan for a 401k. During the speech, the speaker must have "revealed" aspects about his four different marriages at least 30 times. To this day I really couldn't tell you anything about the different funds that one could use as part of their 401k plan, but I can vividly recall aspects of each of this guy's marriages. This was a clear case of TMI: too-much-information. No the speech wasn't boring, but the amount of personal information that was being shared overpowered the message. There's got to be a balance.

So Where Do You Draw The Line?

All of us desperately want to avoid giving boring speeches. However, we also want to make sure that our speeches have an impact – and if we're sharing too much personal information this isn't going to happen. Here are some tips on how to draw the line between too much and too little personal information correctly:

Match Your Speech Type: certain types of speeches naturally lend themselves more readily to having personal information included in them. Speeches in which you are trying to persuade or entertain your audience are great vehicles for more personal information. Speeches to inform are not.

Match Your Audience: Who is in your audience (and why are they there)? If you have a business audience who are looking for ways to keep their business afloat during a severe economic downturn, then your childhood stories are not going to be appropriate. However, if you are speaking to a Garden Club filled with mothers, then perhaps a childhood story might be the perfect way to establish rapport.

Stay On Topic: Sharing personal information just because it makes a great story (like my 401k presenter did) is a bad idea. You need to make sure that the story ties in with what your speech is all about. If it doesn't, then skip it.

Listen To Your Audience: In the end, it all comes down to what your audience wants to hear. If, while you are giving your speech, you start to detect that your audience is not staying with you, then cut back on the personal information and instead focus on your core content.

Final Thoughts

This is one of those tough areas where you are going to have to rely on your speaker's judgment. Sometimes you'll get it right and sometimes you might be off the mark and include either too little or too much personal information in one of your speeches. However, keep at it and refine each speech the next time you give it. In the end, you'll know how much personal information to include in order to be able to intimately connect with your audience and make an lasting impact in their lives.

Chapter 12

How To Appeal To Your Audience: Greek Lessons

Chapter 12: How To Appeal To Your Audience: Greek Lessons

If you are going to go to the effort of creating and delivering a speech, doesn't it make sense that you'd want to be able to reach your audience and somehow appeal to them? No matter if you are trying to persuade them or educate them, ultimately the goal is find a way to successfully appeal to them. Good news – how to do this has been known for the past 2,500 years!

Aristotle Knew Everything

Robert Oliver has been doing some research and he's discovered that most of what we are trying to accomplish in our speeches today is exactly what the ancient Greeks were trying to do oh so long ago.

You've got to remember that there for a while the Greeks were at the height of their civilization – they had invented democracy and really had nothing else to do but sit around and give speeches. This meant that they got interested in what made a speech appeal to an audience (and what didn't).

Having listened to a countless number of speeches, Aristotle came to the realization that there is no such thing as a "one size fits all" speech. Instead, if you want to appeal to a given audience, you're going to have to pick the type of speech that will work for that audience. Thankfully, Aristotle went one step further and discovered the three different types of speeches that worked best for appealing to your audience: logical, pathetic, and ethical.

- The Logical appeal is an appeal to reason that you use to convince your audience that your argument is correct.

- The Pathetic appeal is an appeal that works on the emotions of the judges themselves.

- The Ethical appeal involves playing on the audience's sense of admiration for you.

How To Arrange A Speech To Maximize Your Appeal

Just picking the correct type of speech to use in order to appeal to your audience isn't enough. You've got to take it one step further. It turns out that how you arrange your speech will have a big impact on your ability to reach and convince your audience.

Once again Aristotle found that there were three basic ways to arrange your speech. Each one was a powerful tool – you just had to pick which would work best with your speech and your audience. Aristotle's suggestions for the three ways to arrange a speech in order to win your audience over are:

- **The Narrative**: this is the story format that all of us Accidental Communicators know and love. It doesn't always have to be a "Once upon a time…" story, rather it can take the form of a parable, an anecdote, a story that is well known to your audience, or even a personal story.

- **Linear Argument**: this is the classic courtroom drama style where the facts are laid out from start to finish where a final conclusion is reached. One point to remember here is that the if you are going to use this arrangement style, then just like a jury your audience is going to have to become and stay fully engaged.

- **Dialetic**: this is just a big word for a compare and contrast story. You lay out your argument step-by-step but at each step you compare your way to another way to show why your way is better. Careful – if you don't watch out, this can slide into a negative presentation. Just a note: Aristotle thought that this was the most effective way to present information.

Final Thoughts

As though giving a speech isn't hard enough by itself, if you want to make an impact on your audience then you've got to design your speech correctly. Aristotle had the time back in the day to think about what worked.

His three types of arguments as well as his understanding of how to arrange your speech in order to appeal to your audience still work today. Listen to what the guy from Greece is trying to tell us and you'll be able to intimately connect with your audience and make an lasting impact in their lives.

It's from the forge of failure that the steel of success is formed.

Hard Work Does Not Guarantee Success, But Success Does Not Happen Without Hard Work.

- Dr. Jim Anderson

Create Speeches That Motivate Your Audiences And Get Your Message Heard!

Dr. Jim Anderson is available to provide training and coaching on the topics that are the most important to people who have to speak in public: how can I create a speech that people want to hear and how can I deliver in a way that will allow me to connect with my audience and get my point across to them?

Dr. Anderson believes that in order to both learn and remember what he says, speakers need to laugh. Each one of his speeches is full of fun and humor so that what he says "sticks" with everyone.

Dr. Anderson's Public Speaking Training Includes:

1. How to plan your next speech: pick your purpose and understand your audience.
2. What's the best way to get PowerPoint and Keynote to work with you, not against you?
3. What do you need to do when you are presenting in order to truly connect with your audience?

Dr. Jim Anderson presents over 100 speeches per year. To invite Dr. Anderson to speak at your event, contact him at:

Phone: 813-418-6970 or
Email: jim@BlueElephantConsulting.com

Blue
Elephant
Consulting
Speaking Negotiating Managing Marketing

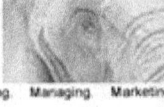

Photo Credits:

Cover - By: Flood G.
https://www.flickr.com/photos/_flood_/

Chapter 1 - By: Het Nieuwe Instituut
https://www.flickr.com/photos/thenewinstitute/

Chapter 2 – By: Oracle PR
https://www.flickr.com/photos/oracle_images/

Chapter 3- By: Mademoiselle -M-
https://www.flickr.com/photos/62594877@N06/

Chapter 4 – By: Mr.Lobo
https://www.flickr.com/photos/mrlobo/

Chapter 5 – By: Light Brigading
https://www.flickr.com/photos/40969298@N05/

Chapter 6 – By: mendhak
https://www.flickr.com/photos/mendhak/

Chapter 7 – By: Pinterest
https://www.pinterest.com/pin/238127899019516110/

Chapter 8 – By: Chad Kainz
https://www.flickr.com/photos/smaedli/

Chapter 9 – By: Dani Latorre
https://www.flickr.com/photos/dlato/

Chapter 10 – By; Flicker
http://stock-clip.com/video-footage/flicker+free/2

Chapter 11 – By: Vertical Response
http://www.verticalresponse.com/blog/the-411-on-pinterest-secret-boards/

Chapter 12 – By: Pinterest
https://www.pinterest.com/pin/495958977692014263/

Other Books By The Author

Product Management

- How Product Managers Can Learn To Understand Their Customers: Techniques For Product Managers To Better Understand What Their Customers Really Want

- Product Management Secrets: Techniques For Product Managers To Boost Product Sales And Increase Customer Satisfaction

- Product Development Lessons For Product Managers: How Product Managers Can Create Successful Products

- Customer Lessons For Product Managers: Techniques For Product Managers To Better Understand What Their Customers Really Want

- Product Failure Lessons For Product Managers: Examples Of Products That Have Failed For Product Managers To Learn From

- Communication Skills For Product Managers: The Communication Skills That Product Managers Need To Know How To Use In Order To Have A Successful Product

- How To Have A Successful Product Manager Career: The Things That You Need To Be Doing TODAY In Order To Have A Successful Product Manager Career

- Product Manager Product Success: How to keep your product on track and make it become a success

Public Speaking

- Secrets To Organizing A Speech For Maximum Impact: How to put together a speech that will capture and hold your audience's attention

- How To Become A Better Speaker By Changing How You Speak: Change techniques that will transform a speech into a memorable event

- How To Give A Great Presentation: Presentation techniques that will transform a speech into a memorable event

- How To Rehearse In Order To Give The Perfect Speech: How to effectively rehearse your next speech to that your message be remembered forever!

- Secrets To Creating The Perfect Speech: How to create a speech that will make your message be remembered forever!

- Secrets To Organizing The Perfect Speech: How to organize the best speech of your life!

- Secrets To Planning The Perfect Speech: How to plan to give the best speech of your life

- How To Show What You Mean During A Presentation: How to use visual techniques to transform a speech into a memorable event

CIO Skills

- What CIOs Need To Know About Working With Partners: Techniques For CIOs To Use In Order To Be Able To Successfully Work With Partners

- Critical CIO Management Skills: Decision Making Skills That Every CIO Needs To Have In Order To Be Able To Make The Right Choices

- How CIOs Can Make Innovation Happen: Tips And Techniques For CIOs To Use In Order To Make Innovation Happen In Their IT Department

- CIO Communication Skills Secrets: Tips And Techniques For CIOs To Use In Order To Become Better Communicators

- Managing Your CIO Career: Steps That CIOs Have To Take In Order To Have A Long And Successful Career

- CIO Business Skills: How CIOs can work effectively with the rest of the company!

IT Manager Skills

- Growing Your CIO Career: How CIOs Can Work With The Entire Company In Order To Be Successful

- How IT Managers Can Make Innovation Happen: Tips And Techniques For IT Managers To Use In Order To Make Innovation Happen In Their Teams

- Staffing Skills IT Managers Must Have: Tips And Techniques That IT Managers Can Use In Order To Correctly Staff Their Teams

- Secrets Of Effective Leadership For IT Managers: Tips And Techniques That IT Managers Can Use In Order To Develop Leadership Skills

- IT Manager Career Secrets: Tips And Techniques That IT Managers Can Use In Order To Have A Successful Career

- IT Manager Budgeting Skills: How IT Managers Can Request, Manage, Use, And Track Their Funding

- Secrets Of Managing Budgets: What IT Managers Need To Know In Order To Understand How Their Company Uses Money

Negotiating

- Learn How To Signal In Your Next Negotiation: How To Develop The Skill Of Effective Signaling In A Negotiation In Order To Get The Best Possible Outcome

- Learn The Skill Of Exploring In A Negotiation: How To Develop The Skill Of Exploring What Is Possible In A Negotiation In Order To Reach The Best Possible Deal

- Learn How To Argue In Your Next Negotiation: How To Develop The Skill Of Effective Arguing In A Negotiation In Order To Get The Best Possible Outcome

- How To Open Your Next Negotiation: How To Start A Negotiation In Order To Get The Best Possible Outcome

- Preparing For Your Next Negotiation: What You Need To Do BEFORE A Negotiation Starts In Order To Get The Best Possible Deal

- Learn How To Package Trades In Your Next Negotiation

- All Good Things Come To An End: How To Close A Negotiation - How To Develop The Skill Of Closing In Order To Get The Best Possible Outcome From A Negotiation

Miscellaneous

- The Internet-Enabled Successful School District Superintendent: How To Use The Internet To Boost Parental Involvement In Your Schools

- Power Distribution Unit (PDU) Secrets: What Everyone Who Works In A Data Center Needs To Know!

- Making The Jump: How To Land Your Dream Job When You Get Out Of College!

- How To Use The Internet To Create Successful Students And Involved Parents

"Secrets To Creating The Perfect Speech"

This book has been written with one goal in mind – to show you how you can create a great speech. We're going to show you what you need to do in order to make your next speech both persuasive and remembered!

Let's Make Your Next Speech A Success!

What You'll Find Inside:

- **WHAT'S THE BEST STORY THAT A PUBLIC SPEAKER CAN TELL?**

- **JUST HOW DOES ONE CREATE A KEYNOTE PRESENTATION?**

- **HOW TO WRITE THE PERFECT SPEECH**

- **PERSONAL INFORMATION: HOW MUCH SHOULD A PRESENTER REVEAL?**

Dr. Jim Anderson brings his 25 years of real-world experience to this book. He's delivered speeches at some of the world's largest firms as well as at many conferences. He's going to show you what you need to do in order to make your next speech a success!

www.ingramcontent.com/pod-product-compliance
Lightning Source LLC
Chambersburg PA
CBHW070942180526
45168CB00003B/1140